Becoming a Citizen

John Hamilton

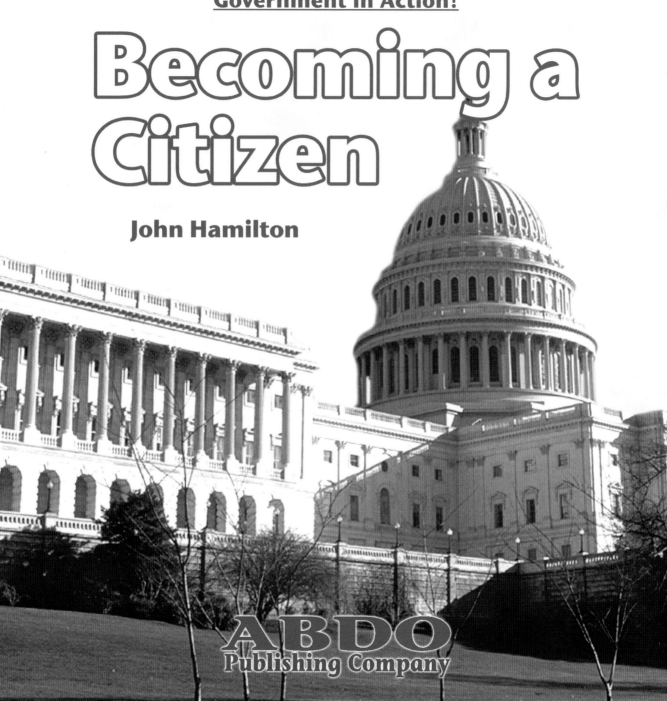

ABDO Publishing Company

visit us at
www.abdopub.com

Published by ABDO Publishing Company, 4940 Viking Drive, Edina, Minnesota 55435.
Copyright © 2005 by Abdo Consulting Group, Inc. International copyrights reserved in all countries. No part of this book may be reproduced in any form without written permission from the publisher. The Checkerboard Library™ is a trademark and logo of ABDO Publishing Company.

Printed in the United States.

Cover Photos: Corbis, Getty Images
Interior Photos: AP/Wide World pp. 15, 29; Corbis pp. 1, 6, 7, 8, 9, 11, 13, 26, 27, 28, 31;
     Getty Images pp. 5, 10; Photo Edit pp. 17, 18, 20-21, 24; United States Citizenship and
     Immigration Services p. 19

Series Coordinator: Kristin Van Cleaf
Editors: Kate A. Conley, Stephanie Hedlund
Art Direction & Maps: Neil Klinepier

Library of Congress Cataloging-in-Publication Data

Hamilton, John, 1959-
     Becoming a citizen / John Hamilton.
         p. cm. -- (Government in action!)
     Includes index.
     ISBN 1-59197-642-1
       1. Citizenship--United States--Juvenile literature. [1. Citizenship. 2. Naturalization.]
     I. Title. II. Government in action! (ABDO Publishing Company)

JK1759.H215 2004
323.6'0973--dc22

                                                                    2003069698

Contents

What Is a Citizen?

A citizen is a member of a city, state, or nation. Citizens have rights and **privileges**. Their government protects them. In exchange, citizens have the duty to support their leader or country.

The idea of citizenship began in Athens, Greece. A small number of the city's residents had rights and privileges that foreigners did not. Later the Romans also developed this idea. However, it wasn't until the 1700s that France and the United States created modern citizenship.

Immigrants created the America we know today. The country grants rights and protection to all of its citizens. Many of today's immigrants go through a legal process to obtain citizenship.

Most U.S. citizens have the same qualities of good citizens all over the world. They want justice and truth, and to be treated equally. In return, they feel a responsibility for the common good.

Opposite page: *Even children can go through the process to become U.S. citizens.*

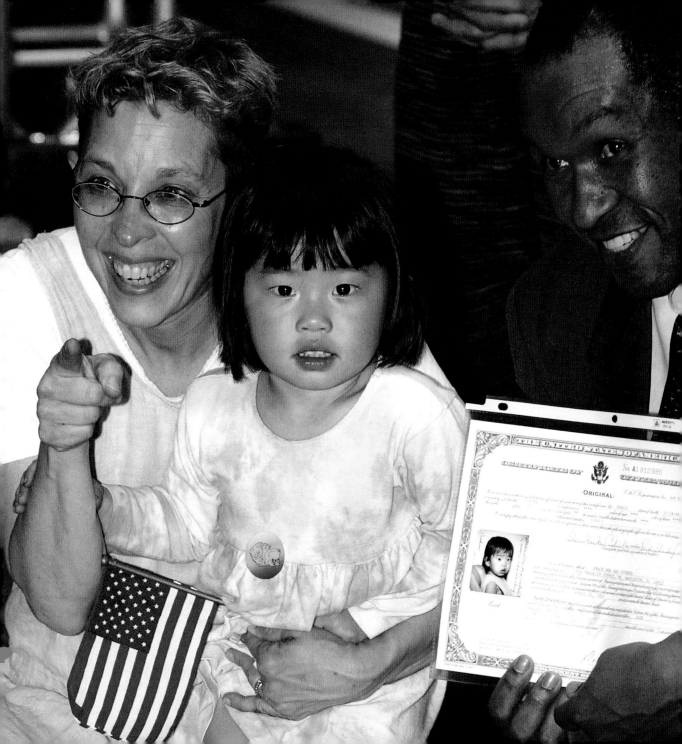

U.S. Citizenship

There are two types of citizenship in the United States. One type is native, which is determined by birth. The other is naturalized, which is obtained by a legal process called naturalization.

A U.S. passport is proof of an American's citizenship while traveling abroad.

Anyone born in the United States or its territories is **automatically** an American citizen. This is true even if one's parents are not citizens. In this case, a person's birth **certificate** is proof of his or her citizenship.

A U.S. citizen can also be born in another country. A baby is automatically a U.S. citizen if both parents are already citizens. If only one parent is a U.S. citizen, he or she must have lived in the United States for at least five years. Two of those years must have been after the age of 14.

Opposite page: *A birth certificate shows a person's place of birth. So, it can prove that he or she is a U.S. citizen.*

North Carolina State Board of Health
BUREAU OF VITAL STATISTICS

STANDARD CERTIFICATE OF BIRTH

1. PLACE OF BIRTH—

County .... Registration District No. **12-70** Certificate No. **264**

or Village ....

Township ....

City .... No. **Grace Hospital** St. .... Ward ....

(If birth occurred in a hospital or institution, give its name instead of street and number)

{ If child is not yet named, make supplemental report, as directed }

2. FULL NAME OF CHILD **Baby Barkley**

3. Sex **Male**	If plural births	4. Twin, triplet, or other....................	6. Premature....... **no**	7. Are parents married? **no**	8. Date of birth **9 - 14 -** 19**37**
		5. Number, in order of birth	Full term... **6**		(Month, day, year)

FATHER	MOTHER
9. Full name **Ned Alexander Parks**	**18. Full maiden name** **Martha Moser Barkley**
10. Residence (usual place of abode) (If non-resident, give place and State) **Morganton**	**19. Residence** (usual place of abode) (If non-resident, give place and State) **Morganton**
11. Color or race **W** **12. Age at last birthday** **24** (years)	**20. Color or race** **W** **21. Age at last birthday** **21** (Years)
13. Birthplace (city or place) **Burke Co. N.C.** (State or country)	**22. Birthplace** (city or place) **Catawba Co.** (State or country)
OCCUPATION **14.** Trade, profession, or particular kind of work done, as spinner, sawyer, bookkeeper, etc. **unemployed**	OCCUPATION **23.** Trade, profession, or particular kind of work done, as housekeeper, typist, nurse, clerk, etc. **Typist**
15. Industry or business in which work was done, as silk mill, sawmill, bank, etc.	**24.** Industry or business in which work was done, as own home, lawyer's office, silk mill, etc.
16. Date (month and year) last engaged in this work ...., 19.....	**25.** Date (month and year) last engaged in this work **3 - 1 -** 19**37**
17. Total time (years) spent in this work	**26.** Total time (years) spent in this work **3 yrs**

27. Number of children of this mother (at time of this birth and including this child) } (a) Born alive and now living **1** (b) Born alive but now dead **0** (c) Stillborn **0**

28. If stillborn, period of gestation	months or weeks	29. Cause of stillbirth	Before labor ....
			During labor ....

CERTIFICATE OF ATTENDING PHYSICIAN OR MIDWIFE

I hereby certify that I attended the birth of this child, who was **Born alive** at **12:05 A.** m. on the date above stated.

(Born alive or stillborn)

{ WHEN THERE WAS NO ATTENDING PHYSICIAN OR MIDWIFE, THEN THE FATHER, HOUSE-HOLDER, ETC., SHOULD MAKE THIS RETURN. }

(Signed) **J. B. Riddle** , M.D.

or .... Midwife

Given name added from a supplemental report ....

(Date of)

Address **Morganton**

Filed **11-5-** 19**37**

.... REGISTRAR.

.... REGISTRAR.

Life in the United States can be very different from an immigrant's home country. To help people adjust, some areas offer classes on subjects such as apartment living, shopping, and using coupons.

However, not all Americans were born U.S. citizens. Many **immigrants** have settled in America. Hundreds of thousands of people still arrive every year. In fact in 2000, one out of every ten people in the United States was born in a foreign country.

Immigrating is a difficult process. It takes a lot of courage to leave one's home country and come to a strange new land. Many newcomers don't even know English when they arrive in the United States.

Deciding to become a U.S. citizen is a huge step in an immigrant's life. Still, these people overcome many obstacles to become naturalized citizens. They know that in most cases, the United States holds the best opportunities and freedoms for themselves and their families.

Coming to the United States can be challenging. Many immigrants must learn English before they can become citizens.

A Citizen's Rights

Arnold Schwarzenegger left Austria in 1968 and became a naturalized U.S. citizen in 1983. In 2003, he was elected governor of California.

Whether native or naturalized, a U.S. citizen enjoys many rights. For example, citizens are protected by their government if they are in a foreign country.

Because the United States is a **democracy**, one of the most important rights is voting. Citizens can vote for local offices such as mayor or city council member. They can also elect state or national leaders such as a governor or the president.

Citizens have the right to run for public office as well. Native citizens may fill any position. Naturalized citizens may run for any public office except president or vice president.

In addition, U.S. citizens are allowed to apply for government jobs. Citizens may also live in the country permanently. And, they can more easily bring family members from other countries to the United States.

Citizens are eligible for federal government jobs, such as mail carrier. Federal jobs offer good pay and benefits.

Protecting Rights

Rights in the United States are granted to all citizens. These rights stem from the U.S. **Constitution**. It is the blueprint of the U.S. government. It contains the basic building blocks upon which all of the country's laws are created.

After the Constitution was written, its creators realized that the basic rights of U.S. citizens needed to be included. In fact, several states would only approve the Constitution if these rights were added. In 1791, ten **amendments** were adopted. They are called the Bill of Rights.

The Bill of Rights protects citizens from the power of the central government. It does this by granting citizens the right to freedom of religion, speech, and the press. The bill allows citizens to gather in peaceful groups in public. And, it **guarantees** all citizens charged with a crime a fair trial.

Opposite page: *Through protest, citizens can exercise their rights to freedom of speech and assembly.*

Immigrants

Only citizens enjoy the many rights provided by the U.S. **Constitution**. To the U.S. government, anyone who is not a U.S. **national** or citizen is an alien. Aliens who come to live in the United States permanently are called **immigrants**.

Often people fear they will not be allowed to live in the United States. Or, they worry the process will take too long. For this reason, some people sneak into the country. These illegal immigrants, or illegal aliens, are not allowed to become citizens. If caught, they are usually sent back to their home countries.

If aliens have **permission** from the U.S. government to live here, they are legal immigrants. Legal immigrants carry identification that proves they are allowed to live in the United States. This identification is called a Permanent Resident Card.

Many people know the Permanent Resident Card as the green card. This is because it used to be green. The card includes information identifying the immigrant.

Many permanent residents eventually become citizens. They do this by going through the naturalization process. Nearly 600,000 **immigrants** were naturalized in 2002.

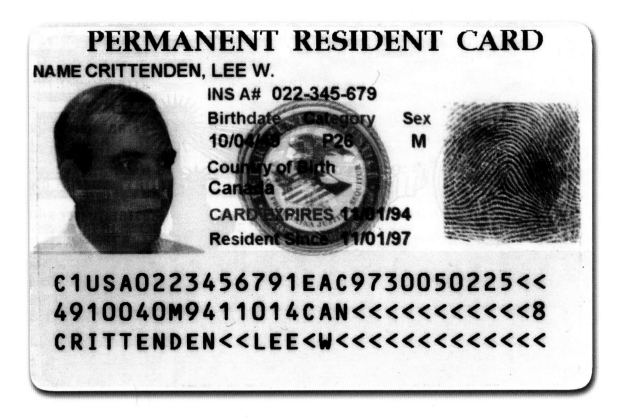

A Permanent Resident Card shows an immigrant's photo and fingerprint. It also has the person's name, alien registration number, birthday, sex, and the date that the person became a U.S. resident.

Who Is Eligible?

In order to go through the naturalization process, **immigrants** must first meet certain requirements. For instance, an immigrant must be at least 18 years old. But, children can be naturalized if adults apply for them.

People wishing to be naturalized must be permanent residents. They need to have lived in the United States for at least five years. Immigrants must also be able to prove that they came to the country legally. This is usually done by carrying Permanent Resident Cards.

To become U.S. citizens, immigrants must have good moral character. This means they must not abuse drugs or alcohol. Lying to get into the country is also unacceptable. Immigrants should also not belong to any group that is against the beliefs of the United States.

Immigrants who want to become citizens must be able to speak and understand English. They will eventually be tested on their English skills. Applicants should also have knowledge of American history and **civics**.

Exceptions

*The U.S. government realizes
that some people may not be able to
do what is asked of them to become citizens.
For this reason, certain people may be granted
exceptions to the requirements.*

*For example, people over a certain age may not need to
know English, and may have an interpreter. Some
people may alter the Oath of Allegiance if they object to
parts of it for religious reasons. Others do not have to
live the full five years in the country. These are just
a few examples. All exceptions depend upon a
person's particular situation.*

The Application

When **immigrants** meet the requirements, they contact the United States Citizenship and Immigration Services (USCIS). This organization is part of the Department of Homeland Security. The USCIS monitors all immigration and naturalization activity.

A USCIS officer helps an immigrant with her application.

The naturalization process can take a long time, sometimes longer than a year. First the immigrant must fill out a form called the Application for Naturalization. The most common is Form N-400. Immigrants can obtain it by mail, over the Internet, or by visiting a USCIS office.

Form N-400 has spaces for an immigrant's name and address, alien registration number, and employment history. It also asks whether an applicant has ever broken the law. Applicants must answer truthfully, or their application may be rejected.

After completing the form, an **immigrant** sends it to a USCIS service center. The applicant also includes two color photographs, a copy of his or her Permanent Resident Card, and an application fee. Some applicants may have to provide other documents as well.

The Application for Naturalization has 14 parts. The last two are completed after the application has been accepted. Part 13 is the applicant's signature at the interview. Part 14 is taking the Oath of Allegiance.

The Interview

When the USCIS receives the paperwork, it schedules an interview. The **immigrant** then has his or her fingerprints taken. This is so the USCIS can check the applicant's criminal background.

At the interview, the applicant swears an oath that his or her answers are truthful and **accurate**. He or she answers questions about his or her background, character, home, job, and other topics.

In addition, the immigrant takes two tests during the interview. The first tests the applicant's knowledge of English. The second includes questions about the government and history of the United States. Applicants study from a list of 96 questions that may be on the **civics** test.

Opposite page: *A USCIS officer interviews an immigrant to see if he is qualified for citizenship.*

If the **immigrant** has passed, the USCIS officer will usually tell him or her immediately. Sometimes a case will be continued if the officer needs more information. If an applicant fails, he or she can often apply again later.

During the naturalization interview, a USCIS officer tests an immigrant's knowledge of both English and civics.

THE TEST

Sample Phrases from the English Test

For the language test, the officer asks the applicant personal questions to test his or her ability to understand English. Then the officer asks the person to read and write phrases about the United States or everyday life.

1. All people want to be free.

2. Citizens have the right to vote.

3. I want to be a citizen of the United States.

4. Only Congress can declare war.

5. The Statue of Liberty was a gift from France.

6. I am too busy to talk today.

7. He wanted to find a job.

8. I count the cars as they pass by the office.

9. She is my daughter, and he is my son.

10. The teacher was proud of her class.

Sample Questions from the Civics Test

1. Which president is called "the father of our country"?

2. Who elects the president of the United States?

3. How many senators are in Congress?

4. What was the forty-ninth state?

5. How many Supreme Court justices are there?

6. What is the capital of your state?

7. Who wrote "The Star-Spangled Banner"?

8. What did the emancipation proclamation do?

9. Where is the White House located?

10. What do the stars on our flag mean?

For the civics test, the officer asks questions about American history and government. An applicant can study from a list of 96 questions to prepare for the test.

The Final Step

Applicants who pass the USCIS interview and test are allowed to become citizens. They next attend a citizenship ceremony. This is the final step in becoming a naturalized citizen. Many USCIS offices hold ceremonies twice a month.

The ceremony often takes place in a courtroom. However, **immigrants** are sometimes naturalized in large groups. In this case, the ceremony might take place in an auditorium or stadium.

During the ceremony, immigrants take the Oath of **Allegiance**. In it, they promise to be loyal to the United States. They also promise to obey laws and fight in the U.S. armed forces if necessary. After swearing the oath, immigrants receive a **Certificate** of Naturalization. They are now U.S. citizens.

A newly naturalized citizen holds his Certificate of Naturalization.

The Oath of Allegiance

I hereby declare, on oath, that I absolutely and entirely renounce and abjure all allegiance and fidelity to any foreign prince, potentate, state, or sovereignty, of whom or which I have heretofore been a subject or citizen;

that I will support and defend the Constitution and laws of the United States of America against all enemies, foreign and domestic;

that I will bear true faith and allegiance to the same;

that I will bear arms on behalf of the United States when required by the law;

that I will perform noncombatant service in the Armed Forces of the United States when required by the law;

that I will perform work of national importance under civilian direction when required by the law;

and that I take this obligation freely, without any mental reservation or purpose of evasion; so help me God.

Duties of a Citizen

The U.S. government was founded more than 200 years ago. It began with the idea that people can govern themselves. This is called **democracy**. It is sometimes called "government by the people."

Serving on a jury is just one of an American's responsibilities.

Through the **Constitution**, the **Founding Fathers** handed down the gift of individual freedoms. Today, U.S. citizens have the responsibility of making sure these rights are not taken away.

Responsible citizens do their duty by voting, obeying laws, and sitting on juries. Americans also defend their freedom by serving in the armed forces. And by exercising their rights, citizens preserve their democratic government for future generations.

More than this, good citizens are involved in their community. They stay informed of current events and issues. Then they vote, keeping Americans true to their **democratic** values.

Another duty Americans have is respecting their fellow citizens. The U.S. government was created so that people could be free to follow their dreams and honor their beliefs. It is why so many struggle to become U.S. citizens.

Some citizens do their duty by serving in the armed forces.

Good Citizenship

Today, U.S. citizens enjoy many rights. But these rights have not come easily. Past citizens sacrificed their lives to protect the freedoms **guaranteed** by the Bill of Rights. Good citizens respect this sacrifice.

One way to show this respect is to observe national holidays. Independence Day reminds citizens of the risks the colonists took in declaring their own nation. Memorial Day and Veterans Day also honor people who fought and died in wars to protect U.S. freedoms.

In addition, good citizens respect U.S. symbols and monuments. The American flag, for example, has inspired

Some citizens show respect for the American flag by reciting the Pledge of Allegiance.

Today, American citizens continue to honor those who have fought for the United States by building monuments such as the World War II Memorial in Washington, D.C.

generations of soldiers as they defended the nation. Citizens recognize this by respecting their flag.

These holidays and symbols represent America's national identity. They honor the sacrifice that went into creating American rights. Respecting these holidays and symbols unites Americans across generations. This unity makes the United States the strong country it is today.

Glossary

accurate - free of errors.

allegiance - loyalty to a country, government, or cause.

amendment - a change to a country's constitution.

automatic - something that happens by itself, without anyone's control.

certificate - a paper that says someone has fulfilled certain requirements.

civics - the study of the function and services of a government and the rights and duties of citizenship.

Constitution - the laws that govern the United States.

democracy - a governmental system in which the people vote on how to run their country.

Founding Fathers - the men who attended the Constitutional Convention in Philadelphia in 1787. They helped write the U.S. Constitution.

guarantee - to make sure or certain.

immigration - entry into another country to live. A person who immigrates is called an immigrant.

national - a person who is under the protection of a country but does not have the official status of citizen.

permission - formal consent.

privilege - a special right, advantage, or benefit granted to a specific group.

Web Sites

To learn more about becoming a citizen, visit ABDO Publishing Company on the World Wide Web at **www.abdopub.com**. Web sites about citizenship and naturalization are featured on our Book Links page. These links are routinely monitored and updated to provide the most current information available.

Immigrants say the Oath of Allegiance together at a Naturalization Ceremony.

Index